A WAY OF LIFE
BE A SAINT!
Union with the Blessed Trinity as Reflected in the Holy Family

Copyright © 1994 by The Apostolate of Christian Renewal. All rights reserved. Printed in the United States of America. No part of this book may be used or reproduced in any manner whatsoever without written permission except in the case of brief quotations embodied in critical articles and reviews. Notwithstanding the forgoing, the Mystical Mass Prayer, Commitment Prayer and order blank may be freely reproduced. For information contact:

The Apostolate of Christian Renewal
P.O. Box 547
Fillmore, Ca. 93016-0547

Phone (805) 524-5890/524-0059 FAX (805) 524-3233

NIHIL OBSTAT:	MSGR. JOSEPH POLLARD, STD. CENSOR DEPUTATUS
IMPRIMATUR:	ROGER CARDINAL MAHONY, D.D. ARCHBISHOP OF LOS ANGELES, CALIFORNIA U.S.A.
DATE:	JUNE 19, 1990

The **NIHIL OBSTAT** and **IMPRIMATUR** are official declarations that the work contains nothing contrary to faith and morals. It is not implied thereby that those granting the **NIHIL OBSTAT** and **IMPRIMATUR** agree with the contents, statements or opinions expressed.

Exerpts are taken from *New American Bible with Revised New Testament* Copyright © 1986 by the Confraternity of Christian Doctrine, 3211 Fourth Street, N.E., Washington, D.C. 20017-1194. All rights reserved.

**This booklet is dedicated to
Jacob and Catherine Zimmer and Family**

CONTENTS

The Logo
The Lay Servants and Handmaids of The Sacred Heart
    of Jesus, Mary and Joseph
    Introduction
    Explanation of Our Name
    Explanation of Our Charism, Spirituality and Purpose
    Questions
    Explanation of the Paschal Mystery:
A Way of Life
    Explanation
    Process of Reflection for Discernment- Preparation- Renewal
    After the Completion of the 40 Days of Reflection
Forty Days of Reflection
Explanation of Consecration and Commitment Prayer
Consecration and Commitment Prayer
Mystical Mass Prayer
Reflections on the Mystical Rosary
    The Joyful Mysteries
    The Sorrowful Mysteries
    The Glorious Mysteries
Evaluation of One's Own Life in Relationship to Jesus' Way of Life
Having Become a Lay Servant or Handmaid
Surrender Song
Grace Before and after Meals
Order Form

THE LOGO
of the Lay Servants and Handmaids of the Sacred Heart of Jesus, Mary and Joseph

The Holy Spirit, the God of Love, is showering His gifts to awaken an awareness, an understanding and a longing to bring to fruition Jesus' prayer for unity at the Last Supper (Jn 17:20-23).

The gifts of love inflame the heart with a desire to embrace the Cross, which is the symbol of the highest and deepest expression of love. *No one has greater love than this, to lay down one's life for one's friends.* (Jn 15:13).

Jesus, Mary and Joseph (JMJ) are the model of love.

† *Let it be done unto me according to Your word. (Mary)*
† *He obeyed and took Mary as his wife. (Joseph)*
† *Not my will but Yours be done. (Jesus)*

Jesus, Mary and Joseph were united in the Incarnational-Redemptive mission with one mind, heart and spirit. Their family life reflected the Life of unity present in the Blessed Trinity. Thus, they are witnesses showing us the way to be a source of unity, and even greater, to be a person living a life of unity with and in the Blessed Trinity and all creation.

THE LAY SERVANTS AND HANDMAIDS OF THE SACRED HEART OF JESUS, MARY AND JOSEPH
+JMJ

INTRODUCTION:

The lay Servants and Handmaids of the Sacred Heart of Jesus, Mary and Joseph is not an organization. Each person is to respond to God in a intimate way as a Catholic Christian.

Our charism and spirituality is reflected in our name.

EXPLANATION OF OUR NAME:

The word Sacred in our name, is used to express the holiness of each person of the Holy Family. Sacred (holiness) is applied to each person in the following way:

- **Jesus**, the God-man, is like us in all things except sin. Therefore, He is all Holy.
- **Mary**, ever-virgin, the Mother of God was conceived without Original sin (the Immaculate Conception) and lived an heroic virtuous life, free from personal sin. Therefore, she is holy.
- **Joseph**, the husband of Mary and a "father" to Jesus is holy because he lived a heroic life of virtue. The Church has proclaimed him to be a Saint, Patron of the Universal Church and Guardian of the Redeemer.

The word Heart in our name, expresses the Unity, Unconditional Love and Mercy of the Blessed Trinity that is reflected in the Holy Family.

- It can be said that the Holy Family is intimately united in one heart, one mind and one spirit.

- United with and motivated by God (Love), the Holy Family comes to know, love and serve all creation through the Paschal Mystery.
- Their way of life reflects the Trinitarian Family Life manifested in our charism and spirituality.

EXPLANATION OF OUR CHARISM, SPIRITUALITY AND PURPOSE:

The charism and spirituality of the Servants and Handmaids is the same for lay people (single/ married/ widowed/ divorced) and those who are called to become brothers/ sisters/ deacons/ priests. To be aware of and understand the charism, spirituality and purpose is a gift given by the Holy Spirit.

Our **charism** is to bring to fruition Jesus' prayer for unity at the Last Supper:

I pray not only for them, but also for those who will believe in me through their word, so that they may all be one, as you, Father, are in me and I in you, that they also may be in us, that the world may believe that you sent me. And I have given them the glory you gave me, so that they may be one, as we are one, I in them and you in me, that they may be brought to perfection as one, that the world may know that you sent me, and that you loved them even as you loved me. (Jn 17: 20-23).

Jesus' prayer for unity is fulfilled in the Paschal Mystery. We are called to live in unity with the Blessed Trinity as reflected in the Holy Family.

Our **spirituality** is to live the Family Life of the Blessed Trinity as reflected in the Holy Family. Our spirituality is manifested through a united common life, in the Paschal Mystery as it is celebrated in each Eucharistic Liturgy.

We offer to our Eternal Father, through the Immaculate and Sorrowful Heart of Mary and the Just Heart of Joseph, in the Holy Spirit, the Body, Blood, Soul and Divinity of our Lord Jesus Christ; from the moment of His conception and embracing the totality of His entire existence; in union with each Eucharistic Liturgy celebrated throughout the world, throughout all time; in atonement for our sins and the sins of the world to bring peace in justice to the whole world.

We offer ourselves, the totality of each person and all creation, with Jesus in union with the Eucharistic Liturgy. This united offering makes our common life meritorious, redemptive and infinite in value. Like Jesus, we become a "living prayer of unity"; a Saint.

Our **purpose**. In the Lay Servant's and Handmaid's "way of life", we are sent forth to bring to fruition Jesus' prayer for unity at the Last Supper (Jn 17:20-23).

The unity of God's family is brought about through the Paschal Mystery in the Roman Catholic Church. Much of our apostolic labor/ministry will be directed towards building up the parish family based on the following:

- We live and share our charism and spirituality so as to bring about the renewal of the person: to help each one become a Saint.
- The family is the heart and cell of society and of the Church. The family unit is best served through the parish family.
- Each person is called to live in union with God, united with Jesus in His Life-offering to the Father, in the Holy Spirit.
- Jesus' Way of Life was one of private and community prayer; fasting and penance; spreading the Good News through catechesis and evangelization; helping those in need (through healing the sick, forgiving the sinner,

banishing the evil spirits and raising people from spiritual death); carrying His Cross; and forgiving with Unconditional Love and Mercy, so that through His redemptive suffering all could be saved.
- United with Jesus, in His Way of Life and offering, we then are empowered to keep the Commandments; live the Beatitudes; and to love and forgive as Jesus has loved and forgiven us.
- Jesus' prayer for unity, flows from the Love of the Holy Spirit and has the power to change hearts bringing about repentance, forgiveness and healing, therefore, building up the Kingdom of God (See Evaluation of One's Life In Relation to Jesus' Way of Life).

QUESTIONS:

What does charism mean?

The word "charism" comes from the root of the word charity (caritas) meaning a gift. Each gift is given by the Holy Spirit to a person for the good of the Church and the world. This gift needs to be accepted and owned by each person who wishes to follow the inspiration and guidance of the Holy Spirit, in the way God desires the gift to be used.

How is this charism (gift) brought to fruition?

This charism (gift) of unity is brought to fruition by the grace of the Holy Spirit to live a life of unity with God, self and others.

This supreme model of unity, which is a reflection of the intimate life of God, one God in three Persons, is what we Christians mean by the word "communion". This specifically Christian communion is the soul of the Church's vocation to be a "*sacrament*". (*Sollicitudo Rei Socialis - On Social Concern*, 1992, #40)

Explanation of the word "intention" as related to becoming a "living prayer of unity"?

The Holy Spirit gifts us with an awareness of becoming a "living prayer of unity", as well as, the reality of our union with all creation in and with the Blessed Trinity through the Paschal Mystery. This unity (communion) encompasses the intimate Family Life of One God in Three Divine Persons and is shared with the Angels and Saints in Heaven, each person in Purgatory, each person in the Body of Christ, and each person in the family of God.

By our intention we offer ourself and our prayers to Jesus. Our offering becomes His offering. Jesus makes our intention a reality by His acceptance and offering of our prayers to the Father in the Holy Spirit. This act of faith is based on the belief that Jesus, the God-man, has the power to do what He wills.

What is meant by the "life of unity" which exists in the Blessed Trinity?

The "life of unity" of the Blessed Trinity consists in the "knowledge of each other, love for one another and service to others". This knowledge and love impels them to serve in unity, through the work of creation, redemption and sanctification. This is how each Person of the Blessed Trinity is united in living their Trinitarian Family Life, in giving service to humanity and all creation.

The indwelling presence of the Blessed Trinity is given to us as a gift at Baptism enabling us to love and respond to God unconditionally with our whole body, mind, heart and soul; and to love our neighbor as Christ has loved us. The gift of Unconditional Love gives us the grace to be merciful as God is merciful. Each person is then capable of asking forgiveness from

God and to forgive self and others in all situations where mercy is needed.

What is meant by a "united common life"?

Through Baptism each person is enabled to live in union with God, self and others in a united common life. A common life includes all that happens in a person's life. United with Jesus in His offering, in each Eucharistic Liturgy, a united common life becomes meritorious, redemptive and infinite in value, thus, reflecting the life of the Blessed Trinity. The Trinitarian Family Life is reflected in the Holy Family. Jesus, Mary and Joseph are our model for teaching us how to live in communion with the Triune God and all creation. Jesus, the source of unity, is the center of our united common life of unity through Unconditional Love and Mercy, to bring justice in peace to all.

- Peace is a God given gift. This gift is given to each person of goodwill, who seeks His honor and glory and strives to live Christ's attitude in mind and heart (the Beatitudes), in order, to love others as He loves us.
- Justice means to give what is due another. Justice is brought about through love. When you love, you will be a just person because you will give what is due to another. When you love in a just manner, you will be given the gift of peace and contribute to the peace of the world. Peace in justice helps you to live the spirit of the law and not the letter of the law. Peace in justice is a gift meant for all by God, to bring to fruition Jesus' prayer for unity.

The greatest act of Unconditional Love and Mercy is the Paschal Mystery. The Paschal Mystery embraces the mysteries of the Incarnation and Redemption.

- The **Incarnation** is the Love of the Father sharing His Beloved Son, the Word of God, with us. The Word of God

(the Second Person of the Blessed Trinity) took a human nature from Mary (the Mother of God) by the power of the Holy Spirit becoming the God-man (Jesus Christ).
- The **Redemption** includes Jesus' Life (suffering, death), Resurrection from the dead, Ascension into Heaven and the Descent of the Holy Spirit. Therefore, each of these mysteries are included in the Paschal Mystery.

EXPLANATION OF THE PASCHAL MYSTERY:

The Paschal Mystery was instituted at the Last Supper. Jesus gave the command, *do this in memory of me* (Lk 22:19). Through the priesthood of Christ Jesus, the Apostles were to bring the Last Supper (Paschal Mystery) to the people throughout the world, throughout all time. The entire Paschal Mystery is re-presented in the Eucharistic Liturgy.

The Kingdom of God becomes present above all in the celebration of the Sacrament of the Eucharist, which is the Lord's Sacrifice. In that celebration the fruits of the earth and the work of human hands - the bread and wine - are transformed really and substantially, through the power of the Holy Spirit and the words of the minister, into the Body and Blood of the Lord Jesus Christ, Son of God and Son of Mary, through whom the Kingdom of the Father has been made present in our midst.

The goods of this world and the work of our hands - the bread and the wine - serve for the coming of the definitive Kingdom, since the Lord, through his Spirit, takes them up into Himself in order to offer Himself to the Father and to offer us with Himself in the renewal of His one Sacrifice, which anticipates God's Kingdom and proclaims its final coming.

Thus the Lord unites us with Himself through the Eucharist - Sacrament and Sacrifice - and He unites us with Himself and with one another by a bond stronger than any natural union; and thus united, He sends us into the whole world to bear witness, through faith and works, to God's Love, preparing the coming of His Kingdom and anticipating it, though in the obscurity of the present time. (Ref. Sollicitudo Rei Socialis - On Social Concern, 1992, #48)

We are confronted with the reality that God is ever-present; we are never alone. With Jesus, in the Eucharistic Liturgy, Heaven and earth are united as one, throughout the world, throughout all time. Jesus, in the Eucharistic Liturgy, has united us as one with the Angels and Saints in Heaven, the persons in Purgatory, the persons in the Body of Christ and the family of God.

Jesus brings salvation to all through the Paschal Mystery! Recall, God has gifted us with a free will. The choice is ours to personally accept or reject Jesus and what He has done for each of us.

- A person can choose to sin, separating himself or herself from God and all creation; becoming a slave to sin and the devil and contributing to the misery and problems throughout the world.
- A person can choose to accept Jesus' Way of Life, and become a "living prayer of unity". United with Jesus, a person participates in bringing blessings, graces and gifts upon all creation.
- Trusting in Jesus, He will strengthen us in overcoming our weaknesses, failings, and faults. He will forgive our sins and give us the gift of Himself.

A WAY OF LIFE
BE A SAINT!
Union with the Blessed Trinity
as Reflected in the Holy Family

EXPLANATION

Each lay Servant and Handmaid is to have as their highest "rule of life", the following of Christ Jesus; as proposed in the Gospel and expressed in Sacred Tradition, Canon Law and the Magisterial teachings of the Roman Catholic Church. Living the Gospel message (the life of holiness) is the fulfillment of Jesus' mission given to us - to be a Saint. We are intimately called to be a "living prayer of unity", reflecting the Trinitarian Family Life, as expressed in our charism, spirituality and purpose.

The life of a lay Servant/Handmaid begins with the desire to respond to an intimate call by God. United with Jesus, we pray, fast, do penance, study, and practice corporal and spiritual works of mercy.

This opens us to the Holy Spirit who increases the gifts of awareness and understanding of Jesus' prayer for unity, to our Father. The Holy Spirit brings about this conversion of heart. We then begin to put God first in our lives, choosing to love God, self and others. The Holy Spirit helps us to take up our cross, forgive our enemies and help those in need. Then, we are able to understand how suffering can be meritorious, redemptive and infinite in value through our united common life with the Blessed Trinity and all creation.

The life of a lay Servant/Handmaid can lead to total surrender and abandonment to the Blessed Trinity. It nourishes the longing to experience intimate union with each Person of the Blessed Trinity and all creation. It deepens the desire for the salvation of each person, recognizing them as a brother/sister in Christ.

When one enters into this intimate relationship, a person begins to grow more fully in knowledge, love and service of the Triune God and His Church. This is a gradual conversion process that opens us to study the basics of our Faith. God can teach us through prayer, study, insight, revelation and locutions, etc., based on authentic teaching of the Magisterium of the Church under a qualified spiritual director/confessor.

PROCESS OF REFLECTION FOR DISCERNMENT- PREPARATION- RENEWAL AS A LAY SERVANT OR HANDMAID

It is most important, that each person (according to their vocation) be flexible in implementing this way of life.

This "way of life" expresses an intimate personal and liturgical prayer life reflecting the Family Life of the Blessed Trinity. This way of life motivates each person to share and sacrifice themselves, in giving God-like service to others according to their ability, gifts and talents. By living this "way of life" we become Jesus for and to others!

EACH DAY

- invoke the outpouring of the Holy Spirit.

- a short meditation on our Faith/Creed is provided for reflection and application throughout the day (use the 40 days of Reflection).

- pray the Mystical Mass Prayer becoming aware of the meaning of each phrase. Experience what it means to offer everything to the Father with Jesus in the Spirit; united with the prayer of our Mother Mary, St. Joseph, each Angel and Saint in Heaven, each person in

Purgatory, each person in the Body of Christ and the family of God throughout the world, throughout all time.

- meditate upon /contemplate the Paschal Mystery through praying the Mystical Rosary. Learn to integrate the mysteries of salvation into your daily life. Choose one mystery each day to meditate upon more extensively. Take the core message of the mystery and recall it to mind throughout the day (use the Reflections from the Mystical Rosary).

- participate in the Eucharistic Liturgy, receive Holy Communion and visit Jesus in the Blessed Sacrament. If you are unable to participate in person, unite yourself spiritually with Jesus by intention, making frequent spiritual communions. Continue throughout the day to unite yourself spiritually with Jesus in the Blessed Sacrament throughout the world.

- it is important to fast. United with Jesus in our fasting, we become aware of and understand poverty and total dependence upon God. Fasting helps to conquer Satan, our weaknesses, failings, faults and sinfulness. It helps us to realize that without God, we can do nothing. We develop an attitude of gratitude for His blessings, graces, and gifts received; motivating us to love God, self and others.

- begin to study the book, *The Apostolate of Christian Renewal*, by Fr. Luke Zimmer, SS.CC.

- begin to listen to the following tapes: *Christian Renewal; Our Father; Love and Prayer; Eucharistic Liturgy; The Rosary; Live Your Baptism; Dignity* and *Vocation of*

Women; Family Spirituality and *Spiritual Development,* by Fr. Luke Zimmer, SS.CC.

AFTER THE COMPLETION OF THE 40 DAYS OF REFLECTION:

- Begin to read the following: *Apostolic Renewal, Family Renewal, Chosen and Cissie.*

- It is important to reread the books and re-listen to the tapes so that the basic mysteries and teachings of our Faith can be interiorized and integrated. This can help us grow in knowledge, understanding and conviction of Jesus' call and Way of Life, that reflects the intimate Family Life of the Blessed Trinity.

- The **Consecration and Commitment Prayer** can be found after the 40 days of Reflection. It may be prayed privately, with a group, or during a special Eucharistic Liturgy celebrated in your parish by the pastor/associate or in your home by a visiting priest (with permission).

FORTY DAYS OF REFLECTION

● **First Day**: We, as Catholic Christians, believe in the great mystery of God, the Blessed Trinity: Three Divine Persons in One God-Father, Son and Holy Spirit. The Blessed Trinity is a Family, ever-present to each other. This Trinitarian Family Life consists in knowledge of each other, love for one another, and service to others. This is how each Person of the Blessed Trinity is united in living their Family Life, in giving service to humanity and all creation.

● **Second Day**: God the Father is the First Divine Person of the Blessed Trinity: the Creator of Heaven and earth. His thought of Himself generates the Word, His only Begotten Son.

● **Third Day**: God the Son is the Second Divine Person of the Blessed Trinity: the Word of the Father. He is equal to the Father in everything. The Son is the Knowledge that the Father has of Himself. The Son, seeing the Father and the Father seeing the Son, Love each other. This Love spirates the Holy Spirit.

● **Fourth Day**: God the Holy Spirit is the Third Divine Person of the Blessed Trinity: the God of Love. He is equal to the Father and the Son. Each Person of the Blessed Trinity is equal in all attributes (all powerful, ever present, all loving, good and merciful).

● **Fifth Day**: The Love which exists in the Trinitarian Family Life motivates God to create and share Himself with others. Their Knowledge and Love impels them to serve in unity, through the work of creation, redemption and sanctification.

● **Sixth Day**: He created the Angels as pure spirits. Each is a person with an enlightened intellect and a free will. The trial and decision of the Angels: The faithful Angels, who chose to be with

God, immediately enjoyed Heaven. The unfaithful Angels deliberately chose to separate themselves from God for all eternity in hell.

- **Seventh Day:** The Love which existed in the Trinitarian Family Life motivated God to create or create-evolutionize the universe: inanimate objects and animate beings (plant life, animal life and human life).

- **Eighth Day:** God's Love brought into being the human family by creating Adam and Eve and uniting them as one (Gen 2:21-25).

- **Ninth Day:** Eve and Adam's sin was one of false pride and disobedience. The consequence of Adam's sin is that all his descendants are effected by Original Sin. Therefore, lack of knowledge, concupiscence, suffering, illness and death affected human nature and all creation. Worst of all, friendship with God was lost!

- **Tenth Day:** God promised He would send a Redeemer in order to restore friendship between God, man and woman. (Gen 3:15)

- **Eleventh Day:** The mystery of the Annunciation: God sent Archangel Gabriel to the Blessed Virgin Mary at a designated time in salvation history. His design was that she remain a virgin and also become the Mother of God. When Mary understood what was being asked, she said: *Behold, I am the handmaid of the Lord. May it be done to me according to your word* (Lk 1:38). Immediately, the Holy Spirit conceived, Jesus, the God-man in and from her (the Incarnation).

- **Twelfth Day:** The great mystery of the Incarnation: The Second Person of the Blessed Trinity, the Son of God the Father, took a human nature from Mary by the power of the Holy Spirit. Jesus, the God-man, has two natures: Divine and human. In His

Divine nature he had a Divine Intellect and Will; In His human nature, He has an human intellect and will. Both natures are united in the One Divine Person.

• **Thirteenth Day:** In God's plan Jesus was to be born into a family. God chose Joseph to be the husband of Mary and the head of the Holy Family. He empowered Joseph to be a "father" to Jesus Christ.

• **Fourteenth Day:** The life of the Holy Family reflects the Trinitarian Family Life. Therefore, Joseph, Mary and Jesus are a reflection and a model for each person and all families in living this Life.

• **Fifteenth Day:** The Holy Family had a profound knowledge of God and each other. They had an intimate love relationship with God and each other. This love was so intimate they became as one. The three hearts were united as one heart (the Sacred Heart of Jesus, Mary and Joseph).

• **Sixteenth Day:** The love of Joseph, Mary and Jesus, united and motivated them to share, sacrifice, and serve God and others.

• **Seventeenth Day:** Each person of the Holy Family fulfilled a unique role in the mission the Father gave to Jesus Christ. Joseph, as head of the Holy Family, husband of Mary, and "father" to Jesus contributed to the fulfillment of the mission of Christ.

• **Eighteenth Day:** Mary, as heart of the Holy Family, wife of Joseph and Mother of Jesus contributed to the fulfillment of His mission. She participated in His hidden and apostolic life and finally during His suffering on the Cross she became the Mother of all, Mother of the Church and our Mother.

• **Nineteenth Day:** The apostolic life of Jesus shows us how to live the Trinitarian Family Life. As an individual, Jesus lived this Life through contact with the Father in prayer, by manifesting love for the Triune God and giving service to others. We are called to live the Trinitarian Family Life.

• **Twentieth Day:** On the last evening of Jesus' earthly life He met with His Apostles for the Last Supper in the Upper Room. During this meal, He took bread and said: *Take it; this is my body* (Mk 14:22). He took the cup and said: *This is my blood of the covenant, which will be shed for many* (Mk 14:24). *Do this in memory of me* (Lk 22:19). The Last Supper is the memorial of the Paschal Mystery re-presented in the Eucharistic Liturgy.

• **Twenty-first Day:** Jesus gave His last will and testimony at the Last Supper. It is His will that we may be one, as He and the Father are one, expressed in His prayer for unity (Jn 17:20-23). Therefore, we are called to love one another as He has loved us; working to bring peace in justice to each person through the Paschal Mystery celebrated in the Eucharistic Liturgy, throughout the world, throughout time.

• **Twenty-second Day:** Jesus went from the Last Supper to the Garden of Gethsemane where He experienced untold agony. It is there that He had to come to grips with the plan of His Father and the weakness of human flesh. The struggle was so great that blood flowed forth from His whole body. He won the victory by saying: *not my will but yours be done* (Lk 22:42).

• **Twenty-third Day:** Meditate upon the betrayal of Jesus, the arrest of Jesus, the imprisonment in Caiaphas' house and trial before Pilate. When Pilate said: Behold the man, they cry was: *Crucify him! Crucify him!* (Lk 23:21). How have you crucified the Lord?

• **Twenty-fourth Day:** Follow Jesus on the Way of the Cross and stand with Mary beneath the Cross as Jesus is crucified. Recall each Station of the Cross and the last words Jesus uttered before His death: *[Father, forgive them; they know not what they do]*(Lk 23:34); *Amen, I say to you, today you will* *be with me in Paradise* (Lk 23:43); *Woman, behold your son...Behold your mother* (Jn 19:26-27); *My God, my God, why have you forsaken me?* (Mk 15:34); *Father, into your hands I commend my spirit* (Lk 23:46); *I am thirsty* (Jn. 19:28); *It is finished* (Jn 19:30). His side was pierced after His death, from which flowed blood and water, symbolizing the death of Jesus and birth of His Church (the Mystical Body of Christ).

● **Twenty-fifth Day:** Reflect upon the first forty days of Jesus' glorified Life, from His Resurrection to His Ascension. Recall His appearance to the women at the tomb, to the disciples at Emmaus, to the Apostles, and then to Peter and the Apostles while fishing. Think of Jesus' forgiveness of Peter and commissioning him to be the leader of His Church by feeding His lambs and sheep; finally the commission of the Apostles (Mt. 28:16-20).

● **Twenty-sixth Day:** Rejoice with the Angels and Saints in Heaven as Jesus ascends to His Father. Rejoice with Him in the reward that was given to His human nature. He is now our Mediator, between us and the Father, in the Spirit. He will be our Judge at the Last Judgement.

● **Twenty-seventh Day:** Jesus said it was necessary for Him to depart because, when He did, He would send the Holy Spirit who would recall all the things that He had taught. In and through the Holy Spirit, Jesus promised that He would be present with His Church down through the ages until the end of time and that the gates of hell shall not prevail against her.

● **Twenty-eighth Day:** On Pentecost Sunday we see the visible manifestation of the Church of our Lord Jesus Christ. Peter, as the Vicar of Christ, the visible head of the Church, calls people to repentance and 3,000 were baptized that day.

● **Twenty-ninth Day:** It is through the Church that each person is called to live the Trinitarian Family Life. This is done in the family, the parish family and in the world. We are called to share and participate in each other's salvation and sanctification.

• **Thirtieth Day**: Each person, from the moment of conception, is a unique unrepeatable gift of God's Love. The husband and wife are co-creators of life with God. Through the Sacrament of Marriage, the husband and wife are to share and participate in each other's salvation and sanctification. If children are given, the parents are to raise, care for, instruct and encourage them to become Saints.

• **Thirty-first Day**: When a person is baptized with water in the Name of the Father, Son and Holy Spirit one enters through Grace more intimately into the family of God and enters into the Mystical Body of Christ, His Church. Sin is eliminated and one is given a participation in the Life of God. God the Father, Son and Holy Spirit dwells within the person. Therefore, it can be said, the Kingdom of God is within. The Holy Spirit, infuses into the soul, the theological and moral virtues and His seven-fold gifts.

• **Thirty-second Day**: Even after one is baptized and has all of these gifts, the effects of Original Sin are still present. Each person is capable of sin. As the use of reason develops a person begins to know right from wrong. One is to be instructed in the Faith and in the great gift of God's Love and Mercy - the Sacrament of Reconciliation. Rejoice and reflect upon this great gift.

• **Thirty-third Day**: Reflect and realize: At the Consecration, the bread and wine become the Body and Blood of our Lord Jesus Christ during the Eucharistic Liturgy. Think of your own First Holy Communion and the great privilege that you have of receiving Jesus each day.

• **Thirty-fourth Day**: Through the Sacrament of Confirmation, a person receives more fully the gift of the Holy Spirit. The gifts received at Baptism are increased. Having received these gifts, each one is called to share by catechizing and evangelizing the Faith. Think about your own Confirmation. How have you lived your Confirmation commitment?

● **Thirty-fifth Day:** Baptism makes us one with Jesus Christ, so as to be Jesus for and to others. A person is called to "live, love and serve" like Him by living the Trinitarian Way of Life. Each person becomes a "living prayer of unity" with God, self and others.

● **Thirty-sixth Day:** Mary our Mother is the model for all people, she lived the life of Jesus. Joseph, did the same, although he followed the Old Testament covenant. He, too, is a model for us. Think about the meaning of Mary and Joseph in your spiritual life.

● **Thirty-seventh Day:** All graces and gifts won by Our Lord Jesus Christ are given through His Church, the Mystical Body of Christ. Each baptized person is a member of this Body and affects the lives of all. Think about the Mystical Body, the Church today. Jesus is the Head of the Church. The Holy Spirit is the Soul of the Church. Mary is the Mother of the Church. Joseph is the protector and Patron of the Church. The Holy Father is the Visible Head of the Church. The Bishop is the lawful successor of the Apostles and the Pastor takes the place of the Bishop in administering the gifts of the Church.

● **Thirty-eighth Day:** In the community of the Church we more easily live Jesus' Way of Life. It is one of private and community prayer; fasting and penance; spreading the Good News through catechesis and evangelization; helping those in need (through healing the sick, forgiving the sinner, banishing evil spirits and raising people from spiritual death); carrying His cross; and forgiving with Unconditional Love and Mercy, so that through His redemptive suffering all could be saved.

- **Thirty-ninth Day:** When living the Trinitarian Way of Life, there will be great obstacles and opposition coming from the world, the flesh and the devil. This is known as spiritual warfare. The growth in holiness (Jesus' Way of Life) is a gradual process; we learn to practice virtue in an heroic degree, thus becoming a mature person - a Saint.

- **Fortieth Day:** Our greatest help in overcoming the world, the flesh and the devil is to be united with Jesus, in His offering in the Eucharistic Liturgy; together with the Church Triumphant in Heaven, the Church Suffering in Purgatory, and the Pilgrim Church on earth. All are united as one in Christ Jesus. United with Him, we offer each act of love, adoration, praise and worship; each act of thanksgiving for blessings, graces and gifts received; each act of reparation for sins that have been, are being and will be committed; and each act of intercessory prayer. This offering, with Jesus, in the Holy Spirit, to our Father is redemptive and infinite in value! The Eucharistic Liturgy is the greatest source of unity, sanctification and salvation! It is through the Paschal Mystery, celebrated in the Eucharistic Liturgy, that we are to build up the Mystical Body of Christ (the Church) and the family of God; to bring to fruition Jesus' prayer for unity and peace in justice to the whole world.

EXPLANATION OF CONSECRATION AND COMMITMENT PRAYER

We wish to explain the meaning of the "Consecration and Commitment Prayer" so that you may understand what responsibility you have in living this "way of life".

Consecration is an act of devotion that consists of the entire gift of oneself. It is a habitual attitude of complete dependence in one's whole life and activity. It implies total surrender in gratitude for blessings received in the past and as a pledge to fidelity in the future.

To entrust oneself is to transfer or commit oneself with confidence to another in order that help may be received to fulfill one's responsibility in living this way of life.

Commitment is pledging oneself by vow, promise or simple resolution to the performance of some action or allegiance to a cause or cooperation with a person or group of persons. The obligation is morally binding depending on the gravity of the commitment and the formality under which it is made.

The spirit of charity, chastity, poverty and obedience is a disposition or attitude in living according to the Gospel's call to live a life of holiness. This does not bind one under the pain of sin. Each one is to live a life of holiness (Jesus' Way of Life) according to one's state in life.

A vow is a free and deliberate promise made to God to do something that is good and that is more pleasing to God than its omission would be. A vow binds under the pain of sin, grave or slight, according to the intention of the one taking the vow. Vows enhance the moral value of human actions. They unite the soul to God by a new bond of religion. Therefore, the acts of religion of a vowed person become more meritorious. The purpose of vows is to invoke divine grace to fulfill one's resolution until the vow expires. Perpetual vows bind until death.

CONSECRATION AND COMMITMENT PRAYER

I, _____
consecrate myself and my family to You, Blessed Trinity, Father, Son and Holy Spirit, and I entrust my family to the Holy Family: Jesus, Mary and Joseph.

I make my commitment as a **Lay Servant or Handmaid of the Sacred Heart of Jesus, Mary and Joseph.** This commitment is to live Your Life, Blessed Trinity, as reflected in the Holy Family at Nazareth, thus bringing to fruition Jesus' prayer for unity at the Last Supper.

I promise You, Jesus, to live the **spirit / or private vow of charity, chastity, poverty and obedience** to Your Church, according to my state of life.

I renew my Baptismal promises to fulfill my priestly, prophetic and kingly role; I renew my Confirmation mission to be Christ's disciple by: catechizing and evangelizing; keeping the Commandments of God; living the Christian virtues; cooperating with the seven-fold Gifts of the Holy Spirit (Wisdom, Understanding, Knowledge, Counsel, Fortitude, Piety, Fear of the Lord) in order to live the Beatitudes (Mt 5-7); forgiving my enemies and persecutors; fulfilling Jesus' commandment, *love one another as I love you* (Jn. 15:12).

I ask You, Jesus, Mary and Joseph, each Angel and Saint in Heaven and soul in Purgatory to intercede for an outpouring of the Holy Spirit's blessings, graces and gifts so that I may live my commitment faithfully until death.

I make this offering in union with Jesus, to our Heavenly Father in the Holy Spirit, in each Eucharistic Liturgy celebrated today and each day of my life.

_____   _____
Signature   Date
Please let us know when you have made your commitment!

MYSTICAL MASS PRAYER

Father Luke Zimmer, SS. CC.

Eternal Father, we offer to You, through the Immaculate and Sorrowful Heart of Mary and the Just Heart of Joseph, in the Holy Spirit, the Body, Blood, Soul and Divinity of our Lord Jesus Christ, in union with each Mass celebrated today and every day until the end of time.

With Mother Mary, St. Joseph, each Angel and Saint in Heaven, each soul in Purgatory, each person in the Body of Christ and the family of God, we offer each act of love, adoration, praise and worship. We offer each act of thanksgiving for blessings, graces and gifts received. We offer each act of reparation for sins that have been, are being and will be committed until the end of time. And we offer each act of intercessory prayer. We offer all of these prayers in union with Jesus in each Mass celebrated throughout the world.

We prostrate ourselves before You, Triune God, like the Prodigal Son with our weaknesses, limitations, and sinfulness asking for Your mercy, forgiveness and acceptance. Like the Publican-tax collector, we ask for mercy and forgiveness. Like the Paralytic, we ask for healing and strength. Like the Good Thief, we ask for salvation. And like Mary Magdalene, give us the gift of Your Unconditional Love of the Blessed Trinity as reflected in the Holy Family.

We consecrate ourselves and all of creation to You, O Triune God: Father, Son and Holy Spirit.

Eternal Father, we ask You in the Name of Jesus, through the power of His Most Precious Blood, through His death on the Cross, through His Resurrection from the dead and Ascension into Heaven, to send forth the Holy Spirit upon all people.

Holy Spirit, we ask for an outpouring of Your blessings, graces and gifts; upon those who do not believe, that they may believe; upon those who are doubtful or confused, that they may understand; upon those who are constantly living in a state of sin, that they may be converted; upon those who are weak, that they may be strengthened; upon those who are lukewarm or indifferent, that they may be transformed; upon those who are holy, that they may persevere.

We ask You to bless our Holy Father. Give him strength and health in mind, body, soul and spirit. Bless his ministry and make it fruitful. Protect him from his enemies and in his travels. Supply for all of his needs.

Bless each cardinal, bishop, priest, deacon, brother, sister and all aspiring to the religious life, especially..., and grant many the gift of a vocation to the priesthood and religious life. Bless all married and single people. Bless each member of our families, relatives, friends, enemies and persecutors especially... Bless the poor, the sick, the underpriveledged, the dying and all of those in need... Bless those who have died and are in a state of purification, that they may be taken to Heaven.

We offer and consecrate ourselves and all of creation to you, Sacred Heart of Jesus, Mary and Joseph. We ask you Mary and Joseph to take us with all of our hopes and desires.

Please offer them with Jesus in the Holy Spirit to our Heavenly Father, in union with each Mass offered throughout all time.

We consecrate ourselves to Archangels Michael, Gabriel and Raphael, and each Angel, especially our own Guardian Angel. We ask in the Name of Jesus, through our Mother Mary, Queen of all Angels, that You, O Heavenly Father, send forth legions of Angels to minister to us: Archangel Michael with his legions to ward off the attacks of the world, the flesh and the devil; Archangel Gabriel with his legions to teach us that we may know and do Your will, and that they may help us to catechize and evangelize; Archangel Raphael with his legions to heal our woundedness, supply for our limitations, strengthen us in our weakness, to overcome demonic depression, to give us joy in the spirit, to protect us in our travels and to supply for all of our needs.

Finally, we ask for the gift of Unconditional Love, that we can live the Family Life of the Blessed Trinity which was reflected in the Holy Family at Nazareth, thus bringing about peace in justice throughout the world. Amen.

Nihil Obstat: Very Rev. Richard Danyluk, SS.CC. Provincial
Imprimatur: Most Rev. Archbishop Roger Mahony D.D.
Archbishop of Los Angeles, Ca., U.S.A.
January 7, 1986

REFLECTIONS ON THE MYSTICAL ROSARY

INTRODUCTORY PRAYER: Eternal Father, we offer to You the mysteries of our salvation in this rosary, in union with your dearly Beloved Son, our Lord Jesus Christ in each Eucharistic Liturgy, celebrated throughout the world, throughout all time; and with Him in each Tabernacle throughout the world. We invite you, Jesus, Mary, Joseph, each Angel and Saint in Heaven, and each person in Purgatory to pray with us and for us.

THE JOYFUL MYSTERIES

- **THE FIRST MYSTERY - THE ANNUNCIATION AND INCARNATION:** Lk 1:26-28

May it be it done to me according to your word (Lk 1:38).

Eternal Father, we offer to You, through the Immaculate and Sorrowful Heart of Mary and the Just Heart of Joseph, in the Holy Spirit, the Body, Blood, Soul and Divinity of our Lord Jesus Christ; from the moment of His conception and embracing the totality of His entire existence; in union with each Eucharistic Liturgy celebrated throughout the world, throughout all time; in atonement for our sins and the sins of the world, to bring peace in justice to the whole world.

- **THE SECOND MYSTERY - THE VISITATION:** Lk 1:39-56

My soul proclaims the greatness of the Lord; my spirit rejoices in God my savior (Lk 1:46-47).

Come, O Mother Mary, into our lives, so that we may intimately encounter Christ through you and be filled with the Holy Spirit. We ask for the grace to go forth to live and share the Good News.

With you, Jesus, Mary, Joseph, each Angel and Saint in Heaven, each person in Purgatory, each person in the Body of Christ and the family of God, we offer to You, Eternal Father, each act of love, adoration, praise and worship; each act of thanksgiving for blessings, graces, and gifts received; each act of reparation for sins that have been, are being and will be committed until the end of time; each act of intercessory prayer. We offer all these prayers in union with Jesus, in each Eucharistic Liturgy celebrated throughout the world, throughout all time.

- **THE THIRD MYSTERY - THE BIRTH OF OUR LORD JESUS:** Lk 2:1-20

We offer our lives to You, Infant Jesus, the God-man, promising You to live the spirit or vows of charity, chastity, poverty and obedience to Your Church, according to our state of life.

We prostrate ourselves before You, Triune God, like the Prodigal Son with our weaknesses, limitations, and sinfulness asking for Your mercy, forgiveness and acceptance. Like the Publican-tax collector, we ask for mercy and forgiveness. Like the Paralytic, we ask for healing and strength. Like the Good Thief, we ask for salvation. And like Mary Magdalene, give us the gift of Your Unconditional Love of the Blessed Trinity as reflected in the Holy Family.

- **THE FOURTH MYSTERY - PRESENTING JESUS IN THE TEMPLE:** Lk 2:22-40

We entrust and consecrate ourselves, everyone and all creation to You, O Triune God, Father, Son and Holy Spirit, at the Offertory in each Eucharistic Liturgy so that our united common life becomes meritorious, redemptive and infinite in value. We express our sorrow and wish to make reparation for each of our sins. We wish to thank You for every blessing, grace and gift You have given us. We ask You for the grace of continual conversion to become a Saint, so that we may be open to the Holy

Spirit, in order, to be transformed to be Jesus for and to others. We ask for the gift to be confirmed in grace and final perseverance.

- **THE FIFTH MYSTERY - FINDING JESUS IN HIS FATHER'S HOUSE:** Lk 2:41-52

Jesus, we ask You to bestow Your mercy upon us sinners, that we may not leave our Father's house. We ask for a special grace for those who have left our Father's house. Help them return home, to find and keep You in their hearts and lives.

Eternal Father, we ask in the Name of Jesus, through the power of His Most Precious Blood, through His death on the Cross, through His Resurrection from the dead and Ascension into Heaven, to send forth the Holy Spirit upon all people.

Send forth your Holy Spirit and we shall be created and You shall renew the face of the earth. Come, Holy Spirit, fill the hearts of your faithful and enkindle in us the fire of Your Divine Love.

THE SORROWFUL MYSTERIES

- **THE FIRST MYSTERY - THE AGONY OF JESUS IN THE GARDEN:** Lk 22:39-46

United with You, Jesus, in the Holy Spirit, may each of us, like You, pray to our Father: *not my will but yours be done* (Lk 22:42).

Holy Spirit, give an outpouring of Your blessings, graces and gifts upon those who do not believe, that they may believe; upon those who are doubtful or confused, that they may understand; upon those who are constantly living in the state of sin, that they may be converted; upon those who are weak, that they may be strengthened; upon those who are lukewarm or indifferent, that they may be transformed; and upon those who are holy, that they may persevere.

- **THE SECOND MYSTERY - THE SCOURGING OF JESUS AT THE PILLAR:** Mk 15:15

In a spirit of silence, we accept all bodily, mental, emotional and spiritual sufferings. We offer them with You, Jesus, in the Holy Spirit, to our Father that they may be meritorious, redemptive and infinite in value.

Holy Spirit, give an outpouring of Your blessings, graces and gifts upon the sick who suffer in body, mind, soul or spirit, the underprivileged and all those in need. Bless each person who is dying, that each may receive special graces and gifts to choose Eternal Life (Jn 17:3) and not eternal damnation. Bless each person in Purgatory, to be quickly taken to Heaven.

- **THE THIRD MYSTERY - THE CROWNING OF JESUS WITH THORNS:** Mk 15:16-20

Behold Jesus, the God-man! Accept Him as our King, our Lord, our Savior, our Brother, our Friend and Bridegroom of the Church. Behold the Vicar of Christ and accept him as the Visible Head of the Church.

Holy Spirit, bless and give an outpouring of Your gifts upon our Holy Father. Give him strength and health in body, mind, soul and spirit. Bless his ministry and make it fruitful. Protect him from his enemies and in his travels. Supply for all of his needs.

- **THE FOURTH MYSTERY - THE WAY OF THE CROSS:** Lk 23:26-31

Jesus, help us to carry our cross and follow You in love, joy and peace. Holy Spirit, bless each cardinal, bishop, priest, deacon, brother, sister and all those aspiring to the religious life.

Grant many the gift of a vocation to the priesthood and religious life. Bless all married and single people.

Holy Spirit, bless our families, relatives, friends, enemies and persecutors. We ask for a growing awareness and love of our role in Jesus' mission, given to us at our Baptism and Confirmation. Help us to develop Your gifts and virtues, so that we may go forth to catechize and evangelize everyone to be Jesus for and to others.

- **THE FIFTH MYSTERY - THE CRUCIFIXION AND DEATH OF JESUS:** Each Gospel

Let us rejoice and be glad! Jesus, our Savior and Redeemer, won salvation and redemption for us. May we accept this act of love by responding in love.

We entrust and consecrate all we have prayed for to the Heart of Jesus, Mary and Joseph. We ask You, Joseph and Mary, together with Jesus, in the Holy Spirit to offer all to our Father at the Consecration in each Eucharistic Liturgy celebrated throughout all time, to bring peace in justice to the whole world.

THE GLORIOUS MYSTERIES

- **THE FIRST MYSTERY - THE RESURRECTION OF JESUS FROM THE DEAD:** Jn 20:1-18

Then the angel said... , He is not here, for he has been raised just as he said. (Mt 28:5-6).

We entrust ourselves and everyone, to all the Angels, especially Archangels Michael, Gabriel, and Raphael and our own Guardian Angel.

- **THE SECOND MYSTERY - THE ASCENSION OF JESUS INTO HEAVEN:** Acts 1:3-14

I am going to my Father and your Father, to my God and your God (Jn 20:17).

Lord, seated at the right hand of the Father, You will come to judge the living and the dead, intercede on our behalf. We offer ourselves to Your Justice, while thinking of our own judgment and eternal life.

We ask in the Name of Jesus, through our Mother Mary, Queen of all Angels, that You, O Heavenly Father, send forth legions of Angels to minister to us. Archangel Michael, with his legions, to ward off the attacks of the world, the flesh, and the devil. Archangel Gabriel, with his legions to teach us that we may know and do Your will; that they may help us to catechize and evangelize. Archangel Raphael, with his legions to heal our woundedness, supply for our limitations, strengthen us in our weakness, to break all demonic depression and bondage, to give us joy of the Spirit, to protect us from our enemies and in our travels and to supply for all of our needs.

- **THE THIRD MYSTERY - THE DESCENT OF THE HOLY SPIRIT:** Acts 2:1-12;40-41

Come Holy Spirit, into our hearts! Give Yourself more fully to us, that we may live the Family Life of the Blessed Trinity, which is reflected in the Holy Family. Give us a growing desire to bring to fruition Jesus' prayer for unity, at the Last Supper:

> *I pray not only for them, but also for those who will believe in me through their word, so that they may all be one, as you, Father, are in me and I in you, that they also may be in us, that the world may believe that you sent me. And I have given them the glory you gave me, so that they may be one, as we are one, I in them and you in me, that they may be brought to perfection as one, that the world*

may know that you sent me, and that you loved them even as you loved me. (Jn 17:20-23).

Holy Spirit, give us an increasing desire to long for Jesus. Help us to make frequent spiritual communions - uniting with Him at Holy Communion in each Eucharistic Liturgy celebrated throughout all time.

- **THE FOURTH MYSTERY - THE ASSUMPTION OF MARY INTO HEAVEN:** Sacred Tradition

Hail, favored one! The Lord is with you. (Lk 1:28).

We ask you - Jesus, Mary, Joseph, each Angel and Saint in Heaven, each person in Purgatory, to pray with us for the Triumph of the Immaculate Heart of Mary, for the conversion of Russia, the reunion of all Christians, peace in justice throughout the world, and for all those in the process of canonization especially for Jacinta, Francisco and Alexandrina.

- **THE FIFTH MYSTERY - THE CROWNING OF MARY AS QUEEN OF THE UNIVERSE:** Sacred Tradition & Rev 12:1-6

Mary, conceived without sin, pray for us who have recourse to you. We believe, you are our mother, sister, friend and queen!

We invite you, Jesus, Mary, Joseph, each Angel and Saint in Heaven, each person in Purgatory, to pray for all religious institutes and all lay associations.

O Triune God, give an outpouring of blessings, graces and gifts upon all benefactors and provide for them generously, according to Your Will. Inspire the hearts and minds of many people to help all religious communities to do the work of God in building up His Kingdom by spreading the Good News of Jesus Christ.

EVALUATION OF ONE'S OWN LIFE IN RELATIONSHIP TO JESUS' WAY OF LIFE

A. **Private Prayer:**
- ☦ Do I look forward to my encounter with God the Father, Son and Holy Spirit in prayer?
- ☦ Do I offer my prayers to God the Father, with Jesus in the Holy Spirit.
- ☦ Do I come to prayer with an openness to the Holy Spirit?
- ☦ How do I spend my time in prayer?
- ☦ Do I really try to meditate?
- ☦ Do I open myself to the gift of contemplation?
- ☦ Do I realize that, in order to develop this deep, intimate love-relationship in prayer, I must relax and be quiet and listen to what the Lord has to say?
- ☦ Do I make the proper preparation to dispose myself for prayer?
- ☦ Is my prayer life spontaneous, or do I have to labor in this relationship. This question is not meant to determine whether you are guilty of fault, but more as a means of evaluation by the spiritual director.
- ☦ Do I seek feelings or other consolations in prayer: Or do I seek the God of consolation?
- ☦ Do I have dryness and inability to express my thoughts in prayer?

B. **Community Prayer:**
- ☦ Do I dispose myself to pray with others?
- ☦ Do I willingly, freely, lovingly, come to community prayer with an attitude of serving Jesus Christ?

- ☦ Do I participate in community praying with a serious attitude of prayer?
- ☦ Do I enter into that community prayer, realizing that I am praying with the whole Mystical Body of Christ and the Communion of Saints?
- ☦ Do I give my whole self, mind, heart, and soul, to the prayer of this moment?
- ☦ Do I realize that, when two or three are gathered in the Name of Jesus Christ, He is in the midst of the prayer community?
- ☦ Do I understand that, when I am praying with others, I am praying with Jesus Christ?
- ☦ Am I willing to pray with another or others, apart from prescribed community prayer exercises?
- ☦ When I am praying in a community situation, do I use this as an opportunity to manipulate or instruct others?
- ☦ Or do I try to bring about the honor and glory of God and building up of the community?
- ☦ Do I listen and make another's prayer as my own?
- ☦ Do I analyze and rash judge the intention of the person praying?
- ☦ Do I try, in my prayer life, to learn the will of God?
- ☦ Do I try to manipulate Him to do what I want done?

C. **Fasting and Penance:**
- ☦ What is my motive for fasting and penance?
- ☦ Do I wish to do this form of penance in a hidden manner?
- ☦ Or do I want to be noticed, to receive praise?
- ☦ Do I realize that this form of prayer is a great tool to conquer the devil, or temptations?
- ☦ Do I undertake fasting on my own initiative, or do I put it under obedience, to really discern God's will?

- ✟ Am I prudent in fasting and doing penance, or is it detrimental to my physical, emotional or spiritual well being?
- ✟ Do I understand that this form of prayer can bring many graces and blessings for the conversion of sinners or for the release of the souls in Purgatory?
- ✟ What form of penance do I perform?
- ✟ Do I understand that it is better to rend one's heart than one's garment?
- ✟ Do I understand that it is better to have interior, rather than exterior penance?
- ✟ Do I graciously accept trials or difficulties which are allowed by God for our sanctification?
- ✟ Do I practice the prayer of fasting of the tongue? (Which means to use the tongue only for loving, charitable, and positive remarks, rather than criticism, judgmental statements and whiplashing, angry words - see St. James' Epistle.)

D. **Spread the Good News:**
- ✟ Do I believe the Good News of the Gospel message, as taught to us by Jesus Christ? Do I really believe that God created all things through an act of Unconditional Love?
- ✟ Do I believe that Jesus Christ is the God-man, our Lord and Redeemer?
- ✟ Do I understand His teachings on faith and morals?
- ✟ Am I convinced that I am called to be a Saint? And that it is possible to do so?
- ✟ Do I live this message in my daily life? That is, am I really trying to be Jesus for and to others?
- ✟ Do I give a witness by my life of what it means to be Jesus for and to others - a true Christian? A true Servant or Handmaid?

- ♱ Do I accept people as they are (where they are at)? And then dialogue with them about the truths of God? Am I really interested in the spiritual welfare of others?
- ♱ Do I believe that the Catholic Christian Church is the true Church of Jesus Christ?
- ♱ Do my words and actions manifest my conviction of this truth?
- ♱ Or do I water down or eliminate certain aspects of the faith in order to please others?
- ♱ Do I share the Good News with others in my community? That is, do I talk about God and the things of God?
- ♱ Do I share my thoughts and reflections and various religious experiences?
- ♱ Do I try to discern the Spirit by listening to others? To determine whether something is from God, the devil, or one's own imagination?
- ♱ Do I emphasize solid, basic spiritual principles, rather than things that may be superficial or accidental?

E. **Helping the Needy:**
- ♱ Do I realize that the world is a vast hospital with the brokenhearted everywhere?
- ♱ Do I realize that I can help to alleviate suffering by my empathy?
- ♱ Am I sensitive to the needs of others when they are suffering?
- ♱ Am I willing to listen, to encourage, to uplift them?
- ♱ Am I willing to spend time with people, to show that I care?
- ♱ Do I respect the dignity, freedom and the right to life of others?

- ✞ Am I willing to use my gifts and talents and even sacrifice to the point where it hurts?
- ✞ Do I pray for all who are in need?

F. Carry the Cross:
- ✞ Jesus said, *Whoever wishes to come after me must deny himself, take up his cross and follow me (Mk 8:34)*. Am I willing to carry my cross?
- ✞ Am I willing to suffer, whether it comes from illness, misunderstanding, persecution or aloneness?
- ✞ Do I realize I am the suffering Christ, when I carry the cross?
- ✞ Therefore, do I realize that I enter into the redemptive mission of Christ?
- ✞ Do I realize that offering my sufferings with Christ in the Eucharistic Liturgy brings graces and gifts to all people in the world?
- ✞ Do I carry the cross lovingly, willingly and perserveringly? Or am I impatient, self-centered, filled with self-pity?
- ✞ Do I realize that when others wait on me in my sufferings I give the other person an opportunity to wait on Christ?
- ✞ Do I have a right attitude about suffering?
- ✞ Do I realize that it is not a punishment from God?
- ✞ Do I see suffering as an opportunity to manifest Unconditional Love for God and neighbor?
- ✞ Do I realize that interior, emotional and mental suffering can be a greater cross than physical suffering?
- ✞ Do I have the mistaken notion that I have to be suffering physically in order to be carrying the cross?
- ✞ Do I realize that living the evangelical counsels of chastity, poverty and obedience is a cross? That these three promises or vows are the nails, which nail me to the cross?

- ✞ Am I willing to be nailed to the cross by taking these promises or vows?
- ✞ Do I realize that when I live according to the vows of chastity, poverty and obedience, I receive double the merit from my actions?
- ✞ Do I realize that I am preparing myself to live such a life?
- ✞ On the other hand, do I realize that when I break the vows, I am committing double sins, one against virtue and another against the vows?

G. Forgiveness:
- ✞ The first words Jesus said from the cross were, [*Father, forgive them, they know not what they do*] (Lk 23:34). Am I willing to forgive anyone who has hurt me, insulted me, persecuted me, misunderstood me or rejected me?
- ✞ Do I forgive myself when I fall into faults or failings or even sin?
- ✞ Do I really accept forgiveness from God in the Sacrament of Reconciliation?
- ✞ Do I really believe I'm forgiven?
- ✞ Do I believe that I still am worthy of God's love?
- ✞ Do I accept the forgiveness of others?
- ✞ Do I again accept others with Unconditional Love as if nothing has happened?
- ✞ Do I really realize that a lack of forgiveness is pride?
- ✞ Do I realize that I cannot help my feelings, that I am as God made me?
- ✞ Do I realize that when my feelings are hurt I can use this as a blessing by coping with the situation and rising above it?
- ✞ Do I see my failings and faults as a means of growth in service to others?

- ✞ Do I realize that there will always be weakness and a tendency to selfishness in myself and others?
- ✞ However, do I open myself to God and accept His help to overcome my own weaknesses?
- ✞ Do I try to understand and encourage others to overcome their faults by my willingness to forgive?
- ✞ Do I praise people rather than criticize them?
- ✞ Do I trust people rather than be suspicious of them?
- ✞ Do I have an understanding of people or do I try to control them?
- ✞ Do I try to bring peace rather than argue, tease or fight?
- ✞ Do I show sincerity and honesty rather than hostility and anger?
- ✞ Do I really forget the past and overlook the mistakes and accept a person and think of that person as having good will?
- ✞ Do I realize that I have to "live and let live"?
- ✞ Do I live in the present moment?
- ✞ Do I realize that all eternity lies in this moment?

All that has been said is cemented together by Unconditional Love (God the Holy Spirit)

- ✞ Do I understand who and what Unconditional Love is?
- ✞ Do I love everyone with this Unconditional Love?
- ✞ Am I willing to bring to fruition Jesus' prayer for unity at the Last Supper (Jn 17:20-23)?
- ✞ Am I willing to become a "living prayer of unity" (a Saint) by becoming Jesus for and to other.

HAVING BECOME A LAY SERVANT OR HANDMAID

Open yourself more fully to a very unique and intimate "friendship in the Lord" with God, self and others through the Paschal Mystery.
- Invite others to live this intimate "way of life" with the Blessed Trinity and all creation.
- Share with others on an individual basis or in a small group.

DAILY PRAYER
1. Eucharistic Liturgy. (See explanation in Process of Reflection ... Each Day)
2. The Mystical Mass Prayer.
3. The Mystical Rosary (5 - 10 - 15 decades). This can be done privately, with the family, or with others.
4. Give service to others in union with Christ. For Jesus said, *Amen, I say to you, whatever you did for one of these least brothers of mine, you did for me (Mt 25:40);* and also *This is my commandment: love one another, as I love you (Jn 15:12):*
- by keeping the Commandments;
- by living the Beatitudes;
- by practicing the corporal and spiritual works of mercy;
- by fulfilling the Precepts of the Church;
- therefore, bringing to fruition Jesus' prayer for unity at the Last Supper (Jn 17:20-23).

SUGGESTED PRAYERS
1. Chaplet of Mercy.
2. Meditate upon/ contemplate the Scripture/ or a Spiritual reading.
3. Liturgy of the Hours.

WEEKLY PRAYER
When Possible:
1. Eucharistic Adoration.
2. Prayer group participation:
   - first, in the family setting;
   - then, in a parish group.

MONTHLY PRAYER
When Possible:
1. Sacrament of Reconciliation.
2. Day of Recollection/Reflection.

ANNUAL PRAYER
When Possible:
1. Retreat.
2. Use the 40 days of Reflection as a renewal of one's commitment as a lay Servant/Handmaid.

SUGGESTED FORMAT FOR A GROUP SHARING
The purpose of the group meeting is to pray together, to study the charism, spirituality and the "way of life" of the lay Servants and Handmaids. Recommended length of meeting is one hour to an hour and a half. The following is suggested when possible:
1. Singing and Praising God. Invoking the Holy Spirit.
2. Spontaneous prayer.
3. Formal prayer:
   - Pray the Mystical Mass Prayer.
   - Pray 5-10-15 decades of the Mystical Rosary. Singing after each five decades of the rosary.
4. Presenting of the charism, spirituality and purpose of the Lay Servants and Handmaids:
   - Taking a portion of a book, article, tape or informal teaching.
5. Individual faith sharing.
6. Individual blessing

SURRENDER SONG

COME LORD JESUS

Come Lord Jesus Co — ome.
Come Heavenly Father Co — ome.
Come Holy Spirit Co — ome.
Come Blessed Trinity _____ .
Make Your home within me(us).

I SURRENDER ALL TO YOU

1. I(we) surrender all to You Heavenly Father;
2. I(we) surrender all to You Lord Jesus;
3. I(we) surrender all to You Holy Spirit;
4. I(we) surrender all to You Blessed Trinity;

(1-4). I(we) surrender all to You my(our) God;

1. I(we) surrender all to You my(our) Dad.
2. I(we) surrender all to You my(our) Brother.
3. I(we) surrender all to You my(our) Spouse.
4. I(we) surrender all to You my(our) God.

HEART OF JESUS

Heart of Jesus, I(we) adore You;
Heart of Mary, I(we) implore You;
Heart of Joseph, ever just;
In this Heart I(we) place my(our) trust.

43

GRACE BEFORE AND AFTER MEALS

Before:
    I have long to eat this Pasch with you because where two or three are gather together in my Name, I am in the midst of you.

    Lord, we believe that You are with us and in us. Help us to see you in each other as we partake of this food which we ask You to bless.

    May this meal unite us in Unconditional Love. We ask this with Christ in union with each Mass which is celebrated throughout the world throughout all time.

    And may the souls of the faithful departed through the mercy of God rest in peace. Amen.

> Heart of Jesus, I/we adore You,
> Heart of Mary, I/we implore you,
> Heart of Joseph, ever just,
> In this Heart I/we place our trust!

After:
    We thank You, Lord, for breaking bread with us and for letting us see you in each other. In union with the Holy Sacrifice of the Mass, help us as we go forth from this table of love to bring this love to others, for You said, *Love one another as I have loved you (Jn 15:12)*.

> Heart of Jesus, I/we adore You,
> Heart of Mary, I/we implore you,
> Heart of Joseph, ever just,
> In this Heart I/we place our trust!

Order Form

☐	Be a Saint! Way of Life ☐English ☐ Spanish			$1.95
☐	Mystical Mass Prayer ☐English ☐ Spanish	12 @		$2.00
☐	☐English ☐ Spanish	24 @		$3.75

☐	The Apostolate of Christian Renewal	$1.50
☐	Family Renewal	$3.00
☐	Apostolic Renewal	$3.00
☐	Chosen	$3.00
☐	Cissie, Sweet Child of Grace, by Anita Morse	$2.50
☐	**All of the above books**	$13.00

☐	Christian Renewal Conferences (3 tapes)	$15.00
☐	Meditations on the Our Father (3 tapes)	$15.00
☐	Love and Prayer (3 tapes)	$15.00
☐	The Mass: The Eucharistic Liturgy (3 tapes)	$15.00
☐	Live Your Baptism (3 tapes)	$15.00
☐	On the Dignity of Women (4 tapes)	$20.00
☐	Rosary Meditations and Praying (4 tapes)	$20.00
☐	Family Spirituality (3 tapes)	$15.00
☐	Spiritual Development (3 tapes)	$15.00
☐	**All of the above tape sets**	$145.00

Shipping Costs

$00.00 - $10.00 ... $3.00 $50.01 - $100.00 ... $8.00
$10.01 - $25.00 ... $4.00 $100.00 and Up ... 7.5% of Value
$25.01 - $50.00 ... $5.50

Materials	$ _____
Shipping Cost	$ _____
Total Cost	$ _____

Make checks payable to: **ACR**

Apostolate of Christian Renewal
P.O. Box 547
Fillmore, California 93016-0547
PHONE (805) 524-5890/524-0059   FAX (805) 524-3233